MUSLIM
DAILY PRAYERS

Compiled under the guidance of

Mr. Elijah Muhammad

Messenger of Allah

To the Lost-Found Nation of Islam

In North America

For the use of members of
MUHAMMAD'S TEMPLES OF
ISLAM throughout
the United States of America

INTRODUCTION

In the Name of Allah, the Beneficent, the Most Merciful, in the Person of Our Father, the Most Honorable Mr. Elijah Muhammad. Peace and Blessings of Allah be upon Him Forever. And may He Forever be One with Allah and the Companions of Muhammad. And We Thank Master Fard Muhammad, who Came in the Person of Allah, in the year of 1930. He is the Manifestation of Almighty God, (Allah). We will remember Him and Praise Him Forever, and we will Honor Him by naming our children after Him for at least one thousand years. And we thank Our Father, the Most Hon. Mr. Elijah Muhammad, for raising the Field Supreme Minister of the New World Nation of Islam, Holy Tribe of Shabazz, Ali Mahdi Muhammad. Peace! Peace!

My Father, the Most Honorable Mr. Elijah Muhammad, who is in heaven, blessed and praised is His name forever, Last God of the Old World and First God of the New World. He told me that prayer was the only thing that will go with us into the New World Hereafter. He said, "In the New World the only thing that will not change is prayer to Allah in the person of Master Fard Muhammad, the Great Mahdi, the Christ, the Messiah."

A Muslim must pray to his creator. He just communicates through prayer at least five times a day and twice at night if he is awake. When you know your creator and submit to him completely you become your creator. God guides you to act like Him through your prayers. When you act like God you are God. You become the creator you serve.

Our Father, Elijah (My God) said, "we are what we eat mentally and physically."

Those of you who eat the truth as taught by the Honorable Mr. Elijah Muhammad, will become Him, His offspring, the Holy Tribe of Shabazz, the Gods and Goddesses of the New World Nation of Islam.

You are all Gods the children of the most high (Psalms 82:6).

Remember that prayer is better than sleep. It keeps you from evil and elevates you in the presence of God.

May Allah's richest blessings forever be upon us all. Peace to you in this world and peace to you in the New World Hereafter.

Peace! Peace! And Love.

Your Brother,
Ali Mahdi Muhammad
Spiritual Leader of the New World Nation of Islam

**In the Name of Allah, the Beneficent,
the Merciful**

As-Salaamu 'Alaikum

Foreword

Here, my beloved people who Believe, is the Book of Muslim Daily Prayers I had promised some time ago to make available to you.

Allah, your God and mine, says in the Holy Quran Sharrieff (29:45): "Surely prayer keeps (one) away from indecency and evil; and certainly the remembrance of Allah is the greatest (force that restrains evil.)"

The knowledge and practice of these prayers will earn you great reward with Allah and bring about great spiritual advancement in you.

Mr. Elijah Muhammad

These prayers, of course, are only a part of your duties as Muslims and as Believers in Allah and His Messenger Muhammad. Keep up your prayers, but be mindful of your other duties as well. Be completely RIGHTEOUS.

At present it is sufficient that you learn these prayers as we have printed them here. Some day in the near future, however, you will learn them in your own language and that of your Righteous foreparents—Arabic.

May Allah bless you and keep you on the Right Path.

ELIJAH MUHAMMAD

Muslim's Oft-Repeated Prayer

The "Fatiha" Printed in Arabic

The Muslim's oft-repeated prayer is the *Fatiha*.

The *Fatiha* ("Opening") is the first Chapter of the Holy Quran and constitutes the Muslim's prayer for guidance.

It is indeed the sublimest of all prayers in any religion. It speaks of Allah's four chief attributes—providence, beneficence, mercy and requital—and exhorts, the believers in Him to seek constantly His guidance and blessings.

******

The *Fatiha* reads thus:

"In the Name of Allah, the Beneficent, the Merciful. All Praise is due to Allah, the Lord of the Worlds; the Beneficent, the Merciful; Master of the Day of Requital. Thee do we serve, and Thee do we beseech for help. Guide us on the Right Path—the path of those upon whom Thou hast. bestowed favors, not of those upon whom Thy wrath is brought down, nor of those who go astray."

Object of Muslim's Prayer

The object of Muslim's prayer is the purification of heart, which is necessary for spiritual advancement.

Benefit of Prayer

Allah promises many blessings to you if you turn to Him in prayer. Nations are no doubt destroyed when they indulge in evil inordinately, and they prosper only so long as their good qualities preponderate.

Daily Prayers

The Muslims' daily prayers are five in number. These are:

1. **THE DAWN** or **EARLY MORNING** prayer (known in Arabic as *Fajr*), which is performed at daybreak and before sunrise.

2. **THE EARLY AFTERNOON** prayer (known in Arabic as *Zuhr*), which is performed shortly *after* the noon hour.

3. **THE LATE AFTERNOON** prayer (known in Arabic as *'Asr*), which is performed around four o'clock in the afternoon, or close to two hours *before* sunset time.

4. **THE SUNSET** or **EVENING** prayer (known in Arabic as

Maghrib), which is performed just *after* the sunset.

5. **THE LATE EVENING or NIGHT FALL** prayer (known in Arabic as *'Isha*), which is performed nearly two hours *after* the sunset time or before retiring.

It says in the Holy Quran Sharrieff (4:103). "Prayer indeed has been enjoined on the believers at fixed times." In other words, it is essential that each prayer be performed at the *appointed* hour.

The exact time for each prayer will, of course, differ from coast to coast, especially when "Daylight Saving Time" is in force. To be sure of the precise hours, therefore, consult your Temple Minister.

Preparation for Prayers

The Muslims' daily prayers are not to be taken for ordinary rituals. You must perform your prayers with utmost sincerity and seriousness, because they represent your Communion with your Maker, Almighty Allah.

To prepare yourself for the wonderful experience known as the Muslim's prayer, and to bring yourself in the right spiritual mood, it is required that you perform an "Ablution," which is done by:

- Washing the hands to the wrists;

- Rinsing the mouth three times;

- Cleaning the inside of the nose with water three times;

- Washing the face three times;

- Washing the arms to the elbows three times (The right arm should be washed first);

- Wiping over the head with wet hands;

- Wiping the ears with wet fingers;

- Wiping around the neck with wet hands; and

–   Washing the feet (the right one first) to the ankles.

In case you take a bath before you wish to perform any of the prayers, "Ablution" as described above is not necessary.

On the other hand, in certain cases, which only your Minister (or, in the case of Sisters, their Teacher at the Temple) can best explain, mere "Ablution" isn't sufficient and a *complete bath* is required before the prayer can be performed.

Significance of "Ablution"

Each part of the Ablution requirement has some significance. For instance, the Muslim washes his hands to "get rid of any evil" they might have committed. This also signifies that the Muslim thus asks Allah to wash his hands in the Spirit of Forgiveness.

"Adhan," or the Call to Prayer

If you intend to perform your prayers in a congregation (group of three or more), a Call (*adhan*) should then be made to the faithful. This consists of the following: (*Only one person makes the Call.*)

Stand erect on the prayer rug or sheet, facing the Holy City of Mecca (East), with your hands upright touching the ears, and recite:

Allah is the Greatest (*Four times*)

I bear witness that there is none worshippable other than Allah (*Twice*)

I bear witness that Muhammad is Allah's Messenger (*Twice*)

Come to Prayer (*Twice*)

Come to Success (*Twice*)

Allah is the Greatest (*Twice*)

There is none worshippable but Allah (*Once*)

The Call to the *Dawn* prayer includes an additional line, which is uttered (twice) after the expression "Come to Success." It says: Prayer is better (for you) than sleep.

Prayer to be Recited After Hearing "Adhan"

"O Allah! The Lord of this perfect call, and of the prayer to be offered! Bestow on Muhammad the means, the greatness, and high dignity, and elevate him in the most exalted place which Thou has promised him. Verily Thou never breakest Thy promise."

Obligatory and the
Traditional Prayers

Each prayer consists of two parts: one
is obligatory (called in Arabic *Fard*), the
other traditional (called in Arabic *Sunnah*);
and each comprises a different number of
"steps", known as *rak'ahs*.

The chart on the opposite page gives
the necessary information pertaining to the
specifications of each daily prayer.

Description of a "Step" (Rak'ah)

A "step" (*Rak'ah*) consists of the
standing, bending, rising, and prostrating
positions. After every two "steps"
(*rak'aks*) there is a sitting position.

Obligatory and Traditional Prayers

Name of Prayer:	Obligatory part: No. of "steps" 2 or *rak'ahs*)	Traditional part: No. of "steps" 2 or *rak'has*)
DAWN	2	2
EARLY AFTERNOON	4	4
LATE AFTERNOON	4	4
SUNSET	3	2
LATE EVENING	7 (Including 3 Witars)	4

The Friday Congregational Prayer: A special Congregational Prayer, preceded by a Sermon, is held each Friday afternoon, replacing the regular EARLY AFTERNOON prayer for that day, wherever facilities for such are available or a mosque exists.

Procedure of the Prayer

After you have performed your "ablution," step on your prayer rug (or a clean folded sheet or large-size towel) and stand erect, facing in the direction of the Holy City of Mecca (which is directly East from most points in the U. S. A.)

Then recite: "Surely I have turned myself being upright to Him Who originated the Heavens and the Earth and I am not from among the polytheists."

Then say: "I hereby resolve to perform two (three, or four, whatever the case may be) "steps" of the Obligatory (or Traditional) part of the (name of) Prayer." This is followed by the raising of hands, accompanied by the utterance of the words "Allah is the Greatest," after which you rest your hands, one over the other, upon your chest.

Then recite the following:

"Glory and Praise to Thee, O Allah! And Blessed is Thy name, and Exalted is Thy majesty, and there is none worshippable but Thee.

I take refuge in Allah against the accursed Satan.

In the name of Allah, the Beneficent, the Most Merciful."

"All Praise is due to Allah, the Lord of the Worlds; the Beneficent, the Most Merciful; and Master of the Day of Requital. Thee do we serve and Thee do we beseech for help. Guide us on the right path—the path of those upon whom Thou has bestowed favors, not of those upon whom Thy wrath is brought down, nor of those who go astray. Amen."

The next recitation comprises a chapter –any chapter—of the Holy Quran. Below is the translation of one, the 112th:

"Say that Allah is One. He is All Independent. He beggetteth not, nor was He begotten. And there is none comparable unto Him."

Following this, utter once again "Allah is the Greatest." Then go into the bending position, and say three times "Glory to my Lord, the Great." Then arise, saying "Surely Allah answers him who praises Him. Our Lord! Thine is the praise."

Now again, say "Allah is the Greatest," after which comes the prostration. While in this position, say three times "Glory to my Lord, the Most High." Then arise, saying "Allah is the Greatest," and repeat the prostration. This completes one "step" (*rak'ah.*)

The second and all subsequent "steps" (*rak'ahs*) are performed by repeating this procedure, except that after every two "steps" (*rak'ahs*) there is an additional position (sitting) to be observed. The recitation for this position is as follows:

"Greetings are for Allah, as also prayers and good deeds. Peace be unto you, O Messenger, and the mercy of Allah. Peace be upon us and the righteous servants of Allah. I bear witness that there is none worshippable but Allah, and that Muhammad is His Servant and Messenger. O Allah! Bless Muhammad and his followers, as Thou blessed Abraham and his followers. And grant Thy favors to Muhammad and his followers, as Thou granted favors to Abraham and his followers. In the Worlds, indeed, only Thou are Praiseworthy and Magnified.

The Holy Ka'ba at Mecca

"O Allah! Help me to be steadfast in prayer and also my children. O our Lord! Accept my prayer. my Nourisher, forgive me and forgive my parents and all the Believers when their judgement is held."

The prayer ends by turning the head, first to right and then to left, and saying "Peace and mercy of Allah unto you!"

Limitations & Exceptions

There are certain circumstances and conditions under which a prayer is unacceptable to Allah. For information about these please consult your Minister (or the Sisters' Teacher).

Looking around, moving or talking during the prayer is strictly forbidden. Even slight movement of the hands is not tolerated, except when such motion is absolutely necessary.

Muslim women need not perform any of the prayers when in menstruation or while in child-bed.

The clothes worn when praying must be clean in every sense of the word.

Holy Quran on Prayer

"So bear patiently what they say, and celebrate the praise of the Lord before the rising of the sun and before its setting, and glorify (Him) during the hours of the night and parts of the day, that thou mayest be well pleased." **(THE HOLY QURAN, 20:30)**

"Keep up prayer from the declining of the sun till the darkness of the night, and the recital of the Quran. Surely the recital of the Quran at dawn is witnessed." **(THE HOLY QURAN, 17:78)**

"Say: Call on Allah or call on the Beneficent. By whatever name you call on Him, He has the best names. And utter not thy prayer loudly nor be silent in it, and seek a way between these." **(THE HOLY QURAN, 17:116)**

A Comment

"Recite that which has been revealed to thee of the Book and keep up prayer. Surely prayer keeps (one) away from indecency and evil; and certainly the remembrance of Allah is the greatest (force). And Allah knows what you do." **(THE HOLY QURAN, 29:45)**

"The verse quoted above invites the followers of all religions to accept the Holy Quran on account of its purifying effect upon life, as the previous scriptures had ceased to effect deliverance from the bondage of sin, which is the real object of the revelation. The verse also lays down the right principle for getting rid of the bondage of sin in the words *the remembrance of Allah is the greatest*, i.e., *the most powerful and effective restraint* upon sin. It is a living belief in the Divine power, knowledge and goodness that restrains man from walking in the ways of His displeasure. A sure and certain knowledge that every evil action leads to an evil consequence, that there is a Supreme Being, Who knows what is hid from human eyes and Whose moral law is effective where the moral force of society fails, and that He is the source of all goodness and it is through goodness that man can have communion with Him, are the only effective restraints upon, evil."

-Maulana Muhammad Ali, in his "Translation of the Holy Quran."

★

First Edition:
February 26, 1957

Published by
UNIVERSITY OF ISLAM
Chicago, Illinois

Procedures for Prayer

"Adhan", or the Call to Prayer

If you intend to perform your prayers in a congregation (group of three or more) a Call (adhan) should then be made to the faithful. This consists of the following: (Only one person makes the Call.)

Stand erect on the prayer rug or sheet, facing the Holy City of Mecca (East), with your hands upright touching the ears, and recite:

Allah is the Greatest (Four times)

I bear witness that there is none worshippable other than Allah (Twice)

I bear witness that Muhammad is Allah's Messenger (Twice)

Come to Prayer (Twice)

Come to Success (Twice)

Allah is the Greatest (Twice)

There is none worshippable but Allah (Once)

The Call to the Dawn prayer includes an additional line, which is uttered (twice) after the expression "Come to Success." It says: **Prayer is better (for you) than sleep.**

After you have performed your "ablution", step on your prayer rug (or a clean folded sheet or large-size towel) and stand erect, facing in the direction of the Holy City of Mecca (which is directly East from most points in the U.S.A.)

Recite;

"O Allah! The Lord of this perfect call, and of the prayer to be offered! Bestow on Muhammad the means, the greatness, and high dignity, and elevate him in the most exalted place which Thou has promised him. Verily Thou

never breakest Thy promise. Surely I have turned myself being upright to Him Who originated the Heavens and the Earth and I am not from among the polytheists. I hereby resolve to perform two (three, or four, whatever the case may be) 'steps' of the Obligatory part of the (name of) Prayer."

This is followed by the raising of hands, palm up and the utterance of the words "Allah is the Greatest" after which you rest your hands, one over the other, upon your chest.

Then recite the following:

"Glory and Praise to Thee, O Allah! And Blessed is Thy name, and Exalted is Thy majesty, and there is none worshippable but Thee. I take refuge in Allah against the accursed Satan. In the name of Allah, the Beneficent, the Most Merciful. All Praise is due to Allah, the

Lord of the Worlds; the Beneficent, the Most Merciful, and Master of the Day of Requital. Thee do we serve and Thee do we beseech for help. Guide us on the right path—the path of those upon whom Thou has bestowed favors, not of those upon whom Thy wrath is brought down, nor of those who go astray. Amen.

The next recitation comprises a chapter— any chapter—of the Holy Quran. The translation of the 112th: **"Say that Allah is One. He is All-Independent. He begetteth not, now was He begotten. And there is none comparable unto Him."**

Following this, utter once again **"Allah is the Greatest."** Then go into the bending position, and say three times **"Glory to my Lord, the Great."** Then arise, saying **"Surely Allah answers him who praises Him. Our Lord! Thine is the praise."**

Now again say **"Allah is the Greatest,"** after which comes the prostration. While in this position, say three times **"Glory to my Lord, the Most High."** Then arise, saying **"Allah is the Greatest,"** and repeat the prostration.

This completes one "step" (rak'ah.) The second and all subsequent "steps" (rak'ahs) are performed by repeating this procedure, except that after every two "steps" (rak'ahs) there is an additional position (sitting) to be observed.

The recitation for this position is as follows:

"Greetings are for Allah, as also prayers and good deeds. Peace be unto you, O Messenger, and the mercy of Allah. Peace be upon us and the righteous servants of Allah. I bear witness that there is none worship able but Allah, and that Muhammad is His Servant and

Messenger. O Allah! Bless Muhammad and his followers, as Thou blessed Abraham and his followers. And grant Thy favors to Muhammad and his followers, as Thou granted favors to Abraham and his followers. In the Worlds, indeed, only Thou are Praiseworthy and Magnified. O Allah! Help me to be steadfast in prayer and also my children. O our Lord! Accept my prayer. O my Nourisher, forgive me and forgive my parents and all the Believers when then their judgment is held."

The prayer ends by turning the head, first to right and then to left and saying **"Peace and mercy of Allah unto you!"**

May Allah continue to bless and protect the believers.

Peace! Peace!

Distributed By:

Elijah Muhammad's
New World Nation of Islam
PO Box 8466
Newark, NJ 07108